EXTINCT ANIMALS OF THE WORLD: KIDS ENCYCLOPEDIA

BABY PROFESSOR

EDUCATION KIDS

In modern times, causes
of extinction have
been dominated by the
activities of humans.

Tyrannosaurus rex lived in the late Cretaceous Period, around 66 million years ago. Tyrannosaurus rex lived in an area of the Earth that now makes up western North America. It was one of the largest known land predators.

Dodos were only found on the island of Mauritius in the Indian Ocean. Dodo birds feed on seeds, bulbs, nuts, roots, and fallen fruits. Dodo birds are related to pigeons.

Thylacines were common across Australia. The Tasmanian tiger is not actually a tiger but a marsupial with stripes. The Thylacine was about 1.8 metres long.

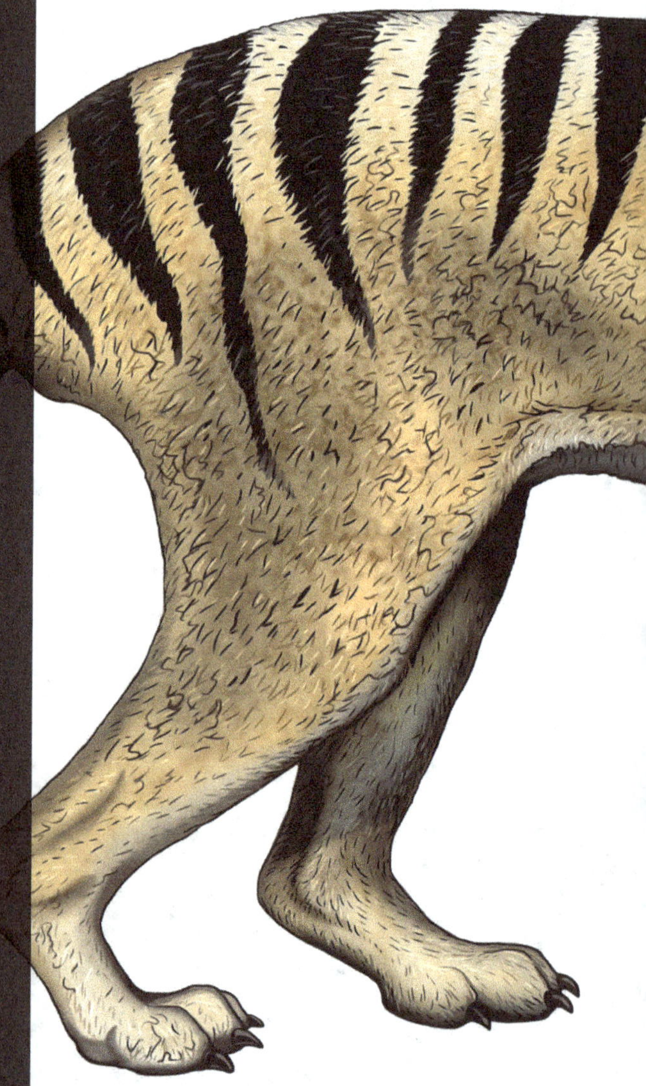

The passenger pigeon only laid one egg at a time. Passenger pigeons once made up about 40 percent of North America's bird population. The passenger pigeon was one of the most social land birds.

The great auk was a flightless bird.
It was 75 to 85 centimetres tall
and weighed around 5 kilograms.
The great auk is often referred
to as the "penguin of the north".

Woolly mammoths are extinct relatives of today's elephants. The woolly mammoth was roughly the same size as modern African elephants.

A saber-toothed cat was a prehistoric cat species. Saber tooth cats were able to reach a height of 3 feet, and weighed around 440 pounds. Their teeth could be as long as 7 inches.

The quagga lived in
South Africa until the
19th century. The Quagga
looked like a cross
between a wild horse
and a zebra. Quaggas
have been reported
gathering into herds of
30-50 individuals and
sometimes travelled
in a linear fashion.

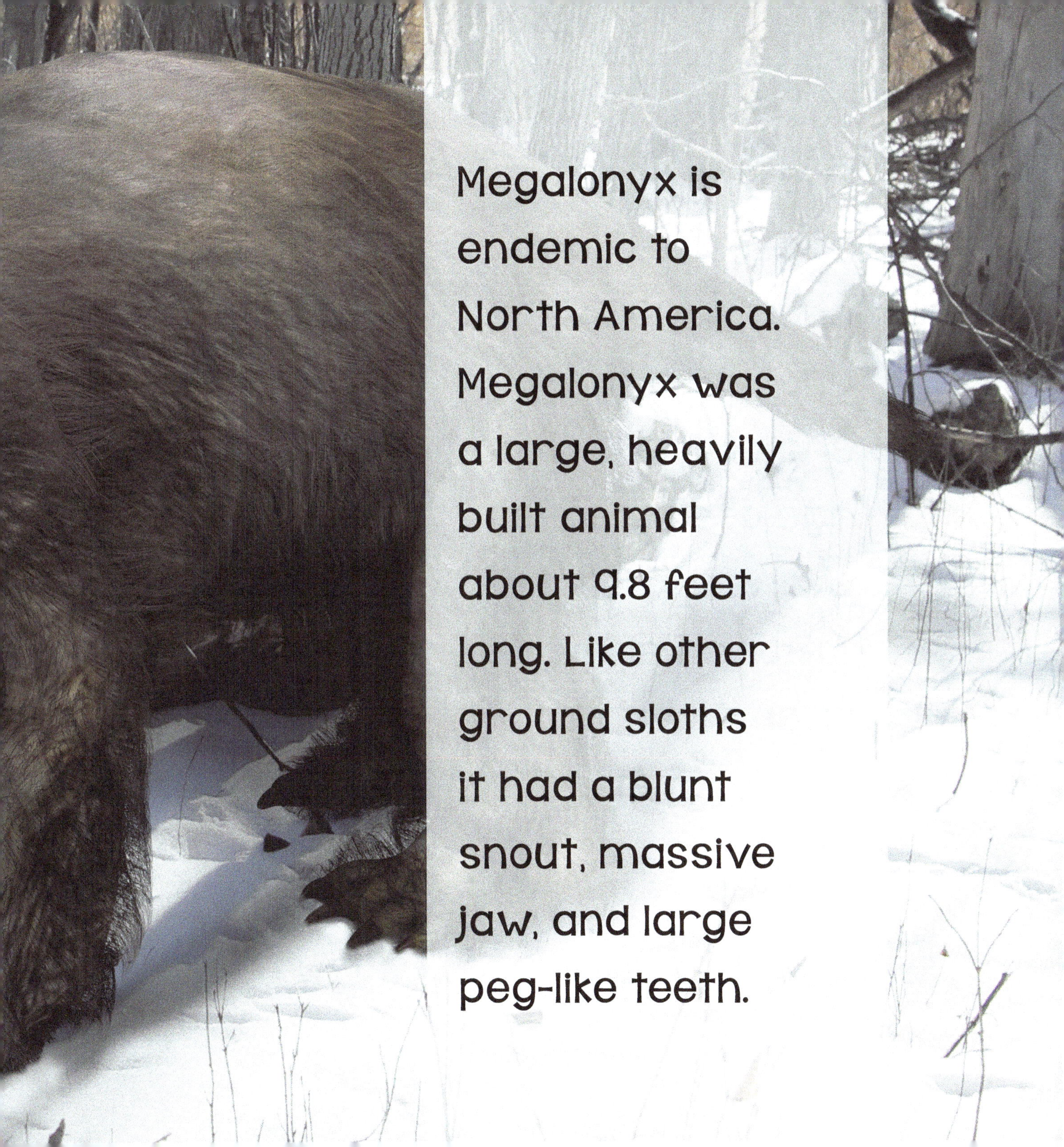

Megalonyx is endemic to North America. Megalonyx was a large, heavily built animal about 9.8 feet long. Like other ground sloths it had a blunt snout, massive jaw, and large peg-like teeth.

The Dire Wolf became extinct about 10,000 years ago when the end of the last ice age occurred. It evolved in North America and later moved into South America. The dire wolf averaged about 1.5 m in length.

The woolly rhinoceros was common throughout Europe and northern Asia during the Pleistocene epoch. It had thick, shaggy fur, small ears, short legs, and a massive body.

The Barbary lion was long considered one of the biggest lion subspecies. Unlike African and Asiatic lions, Barbaries actively preferred forested, mountainous terrain.

Triceratops is a herbivorous dinosaur that appeared about 68 million years ago in what is now North America. Triceratops was comparable in size to an African elephant.

Ankylosaurus
was a heavily
armored dinosaur
with a large club-
like protrusion
at the end of its
tail. Ankylosaurus
measured up to
6.25 m in length.
Ankylosaurus is
thought to have
been a slow
moving animal.

www.ingramcontent.com/pod-product-compliance
Lightning Source LLC
Chambersburg PA
CBHW060149120726
48003CB00010B/3091